THE NEW PHILOSOPHY
OF PUBLIC DEBT

THE BROOKINGS INSTITUTION

The Brookings Institution—Devoted to Public Service through Research and Training in the Social Sciences—was incorporated on December 8, 1927. Broadly stated, the Institution has two primary purposes: the first is to aid constructively in the development of sound national policies; and the second is to offer training of a supergraduate character to students of the social sciences.

The responsibility for the final determination of the Institution's policies and its program of work for the administration of its endowment is vested in a self-perpetuating board of trustees. It is the function of the trustees to make possible the conduct of scientific research under the most favorable conditions, and to safeguard the independence of the research staff in the pursuit of their studies and in the publication of the results of such studies. It is not a part of their function to determine, control, or influence the conduct of particular investigations or the conclusions reached, but only to approve the principal fields of investigation to which the available funds are to be allocated, and to satisfy themselves with reference to the intellectual competence and scientific integrity of the staff. Major responsibility for "formulating general policies and co-ordinating the activities of the Institution" is vested in the president. The by-laws provide also that "there shall be an advisory council selected by the president from among the scientific staff of the Institution."

THE NEW PHILOSOPHY
OF
PUBLIC DEBT

By

Harold G. Moulton

WASHINGTON, D.C.

THE BROOKINGS INSTITUTION

1943

Printed in the United States of America
George Banta Publishing Company
Menasha, Wisconsin

This study was made possible by funds granted by The Maurice and Laura Falk Foundation of Pittsburgh. However, the Falk Foundation is not the author, publisher, or proprietor of this publication and is not to be understood as approving or disapproving by virtue of its grant any of the statements and views expressed herein.

CONTENTS

I. CONFLICTING DEBT PHILOSOPHIES

Two opposing philosophies with respect to public finance exist in high government circles today. The first, which may be called the *traditional* view, is that a continuously unbalanced budget and rapidly rising public debt imperil the financial stability of the nation. The second, or *new* conception, is that a huge public debt is a national asset rather than a liability and that continuous deficit spending is essential to the economic prosperity of the nation. According to this view, the conception of a balanced budget belongs in the category of obsolete economic dogma, the fallacy of which has been clearly demonstrated in recent years.

The *traditional* view is held by the United States Treasury, by the Board of Governors of the Federal Reserve System, by the President, by numerous congressional leaders both in the House and in the Senate, and by many individuals occupying important positions in the administration. The *new* conception is advocated by the National Resources Planning Board, by numerous individuals high in the councils of the government, and by various groups not connected with the administration.

1

To reveal how fundamental is the difference between the old and the new conception of the economic significance of the public debt, a few quotations are essential.

The traditional point of view with respect to the public debt is implicit in all of the Treasury's literature in connection with the sale of war bonds. And it was stated explicitly by Secretary Morgenthau in testifying before the Senate Finance Committee on August 8, 1941, as follows:

The defense program is an absolute necessity. It must be paid for. In so far as possible, it should be paid for now. Borrowing should be kept to a minimum to maintain our fiscal strength. The rise in the Federal debt means merely that the taxpayer's burden is being postponed—that both principal and interest must be paid later out of higher taxes collected at a time when they may be harder to pay and less willingly paid than now. . . .

An all-out tax program will build public morale in an all-out defense program. By reducing the necessity for borrowing, it will strengthen confidence in the impregnable fiscal position of the Government.[1]

In a Special Report to the Congress on December 31, 1940, the Board of Governors of the Fed-

[1] *Revenue Act of 1941,* Hearings before the Senate Committee on Finance. 77 Cong. 1 sess., pp. 2, 7.

eral Reserve System, the presidents of the Federal
Reserve banks, and the Federal Advisory Council
expressed themselves in the following way:

Whatever the point may be at which the budget
should be balanced, there cannot be any question
that whenever the country approaches a condition of
full utilization of its economic capacity, with appropriate consideration of both employment and production, the budget should be balanced. This will be
essential if monetary responsibility is to be discharged
effectively.[2]

In presenting the 1944 budget the President de-
clared that "a debt (of 210 billion dollars) can and
will be repaid. The Nation is soundly solvent."
Chairman Doughton of the Ways and Means Committee says, "the financial integrity of the nation
must be maintained."

The new philosophy, as already indicated, holds
that public finance is really only a matter of book-
keeping, that a rising debt has no adverse conse-
quences, and that without a constantly increasing
debt we cannot hope to have full employment and
prosperity.

The National Resources Planning Board, official
agency of the administration with respect to the
broad field of economic and social planning, in its

[2] *Annual Report of the Board of Governors* (1940) p. 69.

pamphlet entitled *After Defense—What?* holds that financial costs are of no consequence—that if we just go ahead boldly with production everything will be in order:

When we organize for maximum production on the basis of full employment, without being stopped by the costs, we discover, as have other nations, that increased production pays the real costs involved. Doing the job pays the bill. In other words, the central problem is not money, it is manpower, resources, and organization. At last we are beginning to see that finance was made for man, and not man for finance.

The National Resources Planning Board apparently does not believe that an *ultimate* balancing of the budget is essential. In a later pamphlet entitled *Full Employment—Security—Building America,* the Board outlines an extensive "Post-War Agenda." In the section entitled *Plans for Financing and Fiscal Policy,* one finds in the list of issues raised no reference to a balanced budget or control of the growth of the public debt. On the other hand, the Board asks, among other things: (1) What policies should determine the *proportion* of required government outlay which should be met by *taxation* and by *borrowing?* and (2) What special methods of financing, such as non-interest-bearing notes, might be used?

It is evident from these questions that it is assumed that a substantial portion of the government's funds would permanently come from borrowing operations, and that at such time as it became difficult or impossible for the government to borrow the money through the sale of its securities, it might resort to the use of non-interest-bearing Treasury notes—in other words, to the printing press method. It should be made clear that in this document the National Resources Planning Board does not actually recommend the use of non-interest bearing notes; it only indicates that this is a method worthy of consideration.

Of the numerous individuals within the government who are advocates of the new philosophy, the most outstanding are the Honorable A. A. Berle, Jr., now Assistant Secretary of State, and Professor Alvin H. Hansen, special economic advisor to the Board of Governors of the Federal Reserve System and the National Resources Planning Board.

Mr. Berle outlines the postwar requirements as follows:

You would . . . have the government engaged in providing credit or cash for: (1) An urban reconstruction program . . . ; (2) A program of public works along conventional lines; (3) A program of rehousing on a very large scale; (4) A program of nutrition . . .

for about 40 per cent of our population; and (5) A program of public health. . . .

Unless we are prepared to finance the demobilization as well as we have financed the mobilization, we shall be headed at best for a depression and at worst for disorder approaching revolution. . . . The technique of doing the job is perfectly understood. The financial crew that can do it will be on hand and experienced. . . . They have indeed been doing it all over the world, during the wartime economy.[3]

To finance this great program he recommends the establishment of a system of capital credit banks which would make loans chiefly for public enterprises, the funds to be derived from Federal Reserve *credit extensions*.[4] The interest rate he conceives need be merely nominal, because "when the government gives to a banking organization the power to create money, it no longer is necessary to offer an interest rate to stimulate that creation."

Nowhere does Mr. Berle suggest that a balanced budget is necessary or that a continuous growth of the public debt might have adverse effects. Apparently all that is required to make the economic system permanently prosper is to continue indefi-

[3] A. A. Berle, Jr., "And What Shall We Do Then?" *Fortune*, October 1941.

[4] Hearings before the Temporary National Economic Committee, Pt. 9, pp. 4066-79.

nitely a level of public expenditures comparable to—if necessary greater than—that of the war period itself.

The scope and character of Mr. Hansen's conception are indicated in the following excerpts from his various writings. In a signed pamphlet issued by the National Resources Planning Board he expresses himself thus:

Every cent expended, private and public, becomes income for members of our own society. Costs and income are just opposite sides of the same shield.[5]

In other publications we find the following:

We shall come out of the war debt free. We shall have no external debt, only an internal debt.[6]

A public debt, internally held . . . has none of the essential earmarks of a private debt. A public debt is an instrument of public policy. It is a means to control the national income and, in conjunction with the tax structure, to regulate the distribution of income.[7]

[An internal debt] is in fact so different from what we commonly think of as debt . . . that it should scarcely be called a debt at all.[8]

[5] *After the War—Full Employment*, p. 5.
[6] Interview published in *Chicago Journal of Commerce*, June 27, 1942.
[7] Alvin H. Hansen, *Fiscal Policy and Business Cycles* (1941), p. 185.
[8] Alvin H. Hansen and Guy Greer, "Toward Full Use of Our Resources," *Fortune*, November 1942.

That Mr. Hansen believes it is not only unnecessary to maintain a balanced budget but that a
permanently expanding public debt is essential to
prosperity and full employment is indicated by the
following:

> The attack on chronic unemployment by means of
> public expenditures financed by a *continually rising
> public debt* is essentially a conservative proposal.[9]

He suggests that public investment might each
year have to be something like 6 per cent of the
aggregate national income, which would mean
from 6 to 8 billion dollars annually.[10] Elsewhere he
emphasizes the great importance of an expanding
public debt as an investment outlet for the excess
money savings which he regards as a permanent
phenomenon of modern society. (See pages 30-35.)

The new philosophy of debt enjoys considerable
support outside government circles. It has, for
example, long been adhered to by Stuart Chase,
the well-known economic journalist. In a memo-
randum to the staff of the Temporary National
Economic Committee Mr. Chase suggested how

[9] *Fiscal Policy and Business Cycles,* p. 181. Italics supplied.
[10] Interview published in *Chicago Journal of Commerce,* June
27, 1942.

public opinion might be moulded in the right direction through a skillful use of terms. Thus:

Spending is a "bad" word. Avoid it like a copperhead. Talk about *government running expenses* and *government plant*. . . .

If spending must be discussed, always remember that every dollar spent by the government is usually a dollar of *sales* on the books of some business man. Keep *spending* firmly associated with *sales, wages, purchasing power*—all "good" words.

. . . Economy is a beautiful word. Visions of thrifty Uncle Abner. Rolling balls of waste string. Economy however means a *loss* to somebody else—loss of *sales* or *wages*. Keep economy and loss firmly associated.

The National Planning Association, in *Guides for Post-War Planning*, states:

In a money economy this [full utilization of resources] depends upon high levels of currency circulation, in other words high levels of expenditures. To the extent that private enterprise does not do so, government outlay (taxation and borrowing) must fill the gap required to bring total expenditures to the desired goal.[11]

This philosophy has recently been accepted by the editors of *Fortune* and is being currently exploited by them as furnishing one of the primary keys with which to achieve permanent prosperity.

[11] *Planning Pamphlets*, No. 8, p. 23.

. . . The purpose of the federal tax system is *not* to raise enough money to balance all federal outlays. Although a balanced budget may at times be desirable, we never have to have one. . . . Once . . . freed from the obsolete concept of the balanced budget, the larger uses of federal taxes can be creatively explored.[12]

In the foregoing quotations we have been concerned only with revealing how basic is the divergence between the new philosophy of public debt and traditional conceptions. The logic by which the new philosophy is supported will be analyzed in later sections.

[12] "The Domestic Economy," *Fortune,* December 1942, p. 16.

II. THE CRUCIAL ISSUE OF
NATIONAL POLICY

The conflict of views so sharply revealed in the foregoing quotations is the crucial economic issue of the present time. If it be true that the recent experience of this and other countries has demonstrated that there cannot be any financial problem so long as we go ahead boldly with production—that just doing the job actually pays the bill; if it be true that all we have to do after the war is to continue public expenditures at whatever level is necessary to provide full employment, our economic future may be viewed in terms of easy optimism. On the other hand, if it be true that a great and continuous growth of the public debt imperils the financial stability of the nation and undermines the very foundations of the economic system; if it be true that the war debt must be paid, or at least be greatly reduced, and that the Treasury must be "soundly solvent" in order that the nation may prosper and progress, then the mounting war indebtedness and the postwar outlook must be viewed with deep apprehension.

This issue is not one of mere theoretical interest, which scholars may debate in leisurely academic fashion. It is of immediate practical concern to statesmen who must make decisions vital to the nation's future welfare. Until it is settled no unified plans for the postwar world can be formulated.

If we simply lay the issue on the table or put it from our minds because we are unwilling to take the time to think it through, we shall be confronted with ever-increasing difficulties. On the one hand we shall find the spending agencies, where the new philosophy is naturally ascendant, pressing for constant increases in appropriations with which to spend our way into permanent prosperity. On the other hand, we shall find the Treasury striving for ways and means of raising ever-increasing amounts of revenue with which to balance the budget, restrict the growth of the debt, and preserve the credit of the government.

Until this basic issue of national policy is settled, we shall inevitably drift in the direction indicated by the new philosophy—because the money appropriating authorities can hardly be expected to muster sufficient resolution to resist the persistent demands for increased public outlays or to levy sufficiently heavy taxes to cover the appropriations.

The apparently easy way is, moreover, always the popular way. Unless the issue is decided by the process of intellectual discussion, it is likely to be automatically determined by the temper and trends of the times backed by the "educational activities" and pressures of the spending agencies.

III. THE EVOLUTION OF THE NEW CONCEPTION

The new philosophy of public expenditures in relation to economic prosperity is an outgrowth of the disordered economic conditions of the early thirties; but it developed to its present form by gradual stages. In the dark days of the depression, unemployed industrial workers, farmers, and also many business enterprises, were in acute need of financial relief, and in consequence large outlays of public funds derived from borrowing operations were unavoidable. But both political parties regarded Treasury deficits as unfortunate; and the new Democratic administration was especially insistent on the maintenance of sound finance, one of its first acts being to make a horizontal reduction in salaries. Among the many economic innovations designed to stimulate recovery, public spending at first occupied a very subordinate place.

It was not until the recovery of 1933 had failed to reach the stage of prosperity, or greatly to alleviate the unemployment situation, that attention gradually shifted to the use of public expenditures as a positive and primary force in promoting recovery. This shift in emphasis was given impetus by John Maynard Keynes who, on a visit to this country, argued that the stimulating effects of a really abundant outpouring of public funds would prime the industrial pump and thus generate a thorough-going recovery and expansion of private business activity. During the early days of pump priming no one appeared to doubt that the budget would in due course balance itself—as a result of the simultaneous expansion of tax revenues and contraction of government expenditures which would accompany a period of prosperity. When the national income reached 75 or 80 billions, it was believed, budget equilibrium would automatically be achieved. [It should be noted here that Keynes—so far as can be discovered from his published writings—has never contended that pump priming would have to be continued permanently or that an indefinite expansion of the public debt would carry no dangers.]

The next stage in the development of the present doctrine grew out of the business recession of 1937. Beginning about the middle of 1936, there was a very substantial expansion of business, and it seemed that the pump priming was really taking effect. But just at the moment when it appeared

that at last we might be emerging from the mires
of depression the incipient boom collapsed, to be
followed by a new depression. Meanwhile, however, the expanding volume of national income had
increased tax revenues; and, in consequence, by
March 1937 the cash deficit, or to use the new
terminology, the "Treasury's net contribution to
purchasing power," or "net income-creating expenditures," had been reduced to negligible proportions and continued low during ensuing months.

Although this improvement in the fiscal situation was strictly in accordance with expectations,
numerous exponents of the spending philosophy
soon took the position that the depression was
the direct result of the shrinkage in the Treasury's
"net contribution to purchasing power."[13]

Before this time the argument had been that we
should increase public expenditures in periods of
depression and decrease them in periods of prosperity; in other words, that we should have an
unbalanced budget in bad times and a balanced
budget in good times. (In the terminology of the
time this was known as compensatory fiscal action.)
But in the light of the 1937 episode, the doctrine
that deficit reduction—whether due to increased

---

[13] For further discussion, see pp. 40-42.

taxes, reduced expenditures, or a combination of both—is deflationary in effect and will lead to depression became in due time a deeply rooted principle of the evolving philosophy.

It was at this stage that the idea of double and multiple budgeting gained popularity—with capital outlays segregated from current expenditures—without too careful a definition of what might properly be included in capital expenditures. It was about this time that emphasis began to be placed upon the "assets" created by public debts—whether such assets be in the form of tangible properties or intangible services, whether they yield revenues or are simply useful to society. Whatever their character all public outlays are in reality *investments*. From this point it was an easy step to the proposition that all increases in public expenditures represent *income* to someone and that all reductions in public expenditures represent loss to someone; and that "costs and income are just opposite sides of the same shield."

Support for the proposition that continuous public borrowing is essential to full employment and permanent prosperity was also found in three related general economic conceptions: (1) that in a "mature economy" the driving force for private capital expansion no longer exists; (2) that we are suffering from a permanent "excess" of money savings; and (3) that *modern* business enterprises have largely freed themselves from dependence upon the capital markets, financing expansion mainly from internal sources. These underlying theories will be analyzed in a later section.

The full flowering of the new conception was delayed until the war paved the way for an unlimited expansion of public credit. Here, as in other countries at war, the vast increase in public expenditures has mopped up unemployment and given us a great increase in national production. Although precisely the same thing happened in former wars, it appears to be assumed by advocates of the new philosophy of debt that something definitely unique has been discovered during the present emergency. We have found the way to full employment. Moreover, "We discover, as have other nations, that increased production pays the real costs involved."

It should be apparent without argument that the present war experience has merely confirmed what was already known, namely, that a great expansion of employment can be provided by unlimited expenditures of public funds. But neither in this or other countries has the war experience shed any light on the question whether public deficits can be continued *indefinitely* without undermining the financial and economic system. If the conclusion is to be reached that internal public debts are of no moment, it must be justified either by convincing historical or other evidence or by irrefutable economic analysis.

IV. APPRAISAL OF THE NEW PHILOSOPHY

Progress toward understanding in any field of thought is fostered by uninhibited discussion. To this end it is always happiest when the ideas or arguments in support of a proposed policy can be discussed without reference to their authors or sponsors. Unfortunately, this is not feasible in the present instance because the new debt philosophy can be fairly, clearly, and adequately analyzed only in the light of the specific arguments advanced by its principal advocates.

As already indicated, the principal advocates of the new philosophy within government circles are the National Resources Planning Board, Mr. Adolph A. Berle, Jr., and Mr. Alvin H. Hansen. Messrs. Berle and Hansen were key witnesses before the Temporary National Economic Committee. Mr. Berle is author of the plan for a new type of public credit banks; while Mr. Hansen stresses control through appropriate fiscal policies. He has written one volume on the subject and numerous pamphlets and articles. Accordingly, the analysis in the following pages will relate in large part to the arguments of these two writers.

1. Expanding Debt as an Essential for Prosperity

As already indicated, three related general economic conceptions or convictions underlie the argument that a constantly expanding public debt is indispensable to prosperity, namely: (1) that we are suffering from a mature economy; (2) that we have a chronic excess of money savings; and (3) that business enterprises are no longer dependent to any great extent upon the investment markets for funds with which to expand productive capital. The establishment of these three propositions was one of the primary objectives of the investigations of the Temporary National Economic Committee. The depression of 1937 was looked upon as substantiating evidence. The nature of the evidence submitted and the validity of the supporting analysis will be briefly reviewed.

The Mature Economy Thesis

The argument that the United States has recently reached economic maturity and that in consequence further growth (under private capitalism) must be very slow starts with an assumption—namely that economic progress is primarily dependent on rapid growth in population and the opening of new productive areas. Conversely, it is held that a declining rate of population growth and the disappearance of frontiers will check economic growth. The nineteenth century is characterized as follows:

> . . . It was a unique epoch. It was a century of rapid expansion into new territory and it was a century of prodigious growth of population. . . . This one central fact of growth and expansion dominated the whole of economic life.[14]

While it is recognized that technology promotes the opening of new territories and an increase in population, it is contended that the potentialities of science are limited by available productive areas and by the size of the population.

> While technology can facilitate the opening of new territory, it cannot create a new world or make the old one bigger than it is.[15]

Since the conception of economic maturity has elsewhere been analyzed in some detail,[16] no extended statement is here necessary.

[14] Testimony of Alvin H. Hansen, Hearings before the Temporary National Economic Committee, Pt. 9, pp. 3503-04.

[15] Alvin H. Hansen, *Fiscal Policy and Business Cycles*, (1941), p. 361.

[16] See Harold G. Moulton, George W. Edwards, James D. Magee, and Cleona Lewis, *Capital Expansion, Employment, and Economic Stability*, The Brookings Institution (1940), Chap. 9.

It may be noted, however, that the American frontier disappeared more than a generation ago and that the rate of population growth began to decline in the United States as early as 1850. Between 1900 and 1930—the era of greatest economic expansion—the rate of population growth declined steadily. If we look at the world as a whole, the argument that economic growth is checked by the passing of frontiers and declining birth rates finds no more support. Since 1900 no extensive new areas involving large capital expansion have been opened up. The settlement of Manchuria was almost entirely on the basis of very small-scale subsistence agriculture.

The history of Sweden affords good illustration of the lack of correspondence between the rate of population increase and the rate of economic expansion. During the 30-year period from 1900 to 1930, the increase in population in Sweden was 20 per cent, while the increase in production was over 300 per cent. Foreign investments were negligible, expansion being almost entirely internal.[17]

---

[17] It should be noted here that increasing productivity may be the result of more efficient capital as well as of capital expansion. It is true nevertheless that nearly everywhere during the period under review the volume of capital investment was rapidly expanding.

It is an obvious truth that the needs and desires of an expanding population constitute potential markets for the sale of goods and services. But it is equally true that the unfulfilled wants and desires of the existing population constitute potential markets. If the economic system is operated so as to expand consuming power in proportion to the increase in productive power, there is no reason why a slowly increasing, or stationary, population should check industrial expansion. And so long as a large proportion of our population is "ill-housed, ill-clothed, and ill-fed," it is not difficult to determine the kinds of additional production which the population most needs.

Curiously enough, it is admitted at one place in the volume quoted above that changes in consumption may be a powerful factor in stimulating capital expansion. The period of buoyant prosperity from 1900 to 1929, and the "radical transformation in consumption habits and ways of living" that took place is explained in the following terms:

This sort of transformation, involving vast investment of capital, can take place without extensive growth, and under the progress of technology we shall doubtless experience again far-reaching revolutionary innovations of this sort. There is, perhaps, inherent in the process of innovation a cumulative tendency which may be described in terms of a geometric progression. That this was true, even of the past century, is at least in part supported by the fact that the percentage rate of increase in per capita real income was approximately a constant. It is, of course, always possible that the rate of technological development may in the future exceed the geometric rate of the past, but here obviously one enters a field of speculation which can be settled only by the actual course of future historical events.[18]

This very strong statement of the relation between rising living standards and capital expansion seems to be a fairly complete answer to the proposition advanced by the same writer that population growth and geographic expansion have "dominated the whole of economic life."

The recent flurry about economic maturity is reminiscent of that of the middle eighties, when a period of acute depression led some observers to conclude that we had then reached a stage of industrial maturity; that the era of rapid growth lay behind us; that productive capacity had outstripped consuming capacity; and that industrial progress in the years ahead would be meager as compared with what had gone before. In a comprehensive survey of the world situation, but-

[18] Hansen, *Fiscal Policy and Business Cycles,* p. 46.

tressed by extensive discussions with both official and private observers in many countries, Carroll D. Wright, United States Commissioner of Labor, concluded that the leading countries of the world

have overstocked themselves with machinery and manufacturing plant far in excess of the wants of production. In England, Belgium, and France the railroads and canals that are really needed have been built. In Holland, the great works are completed; Amsterdam is united to the sea, international communications have been well established. In Italy and Spain the great arteries are provided with railroads. Harbors and rivers are sufficiently developed, and warehouses, water and gas works, tramways, etc., are largely provided for. The Pyrenees and the Alps are tunnelled. In Russia the principal lines of railroads have been built. Germany is provided with a full network of railroads, and the facilities for transportation are in excess of actual needs. Austria is in much the same condition as Germany, and Turkey also has as many railroads as can be used. In the United States the mileage of new railroads constructed has been out of proportion to the increase of products to be carried. The Suez Canal has been built, terrestrial and transoceanic lines of telegraph have been laid, and the merchant marine has been transformed from wood to iron. On all sides one sees the accomplished results of the labor of half a century. This full supply of economic tools is the most important factor in the present industrial depression. The discovery of new processes of manufacture will undoubtedly continue, and this will act as an ameliorating influence, but it will not leave room for a marked extension, such as has been witnessed during the last fifty years, or afford a remunerative employment of the vast amount of capital which has been created during that period. The day of large profits is probably past.[19]

David A. Wells, the eminent business analyst of the latter part of the nineteenth century, reached a similar conclusion:

There is very much that contributes to the support of the idea . . . that the industrial activity of the greater part of this century has been devoted to fully equipping civilized countries of the world with economic tools, and that the work of the future, in this same sphere, must be necessarily that of repair and replacements, rather than of new construction.[20]

These observers, like the present-day adherents of the mature economy philosophy, overlooked the vast continuing potentialities for intensive capital development. In the great new era of expansion which followed, intensive industrialization, together with some new industries, offered larger outlets for investment than had been furnished by the previous period of geographical expansion

[19] *First Annual Report of Commissioner of Labor* (1886), pp. 256-57.
[20] "The Great Depression of Trade," *The Contemporary Review*, August 1887, pp. 291-92.

across wide continental areas.

The capital requirements over the next generation loom fully as large as those of any preceding period. On the basis of projected population trends, some authorities estimate that the United States may have by 1980 as many as 187 million inhabitants. To supply the primary needs of the additional population, and at the same time to raise the standards of living of the entire population, say, 100 per cent, would require a much larger annual capital expansion than we have had during any comparable period in the past. In making this statement allowance is made for the usual rate of increase in man-hour productivity resulting from technical progress. The realization of the production program involved in this expansion would necessitate the employment (on a 40-hour week basis) of a larger proportion of the total population than was employed in 1929.[20a]

Concern has at times been manifested over the possibility that in the future we may lack the accelerating influence which flows from the development of great new industries. As we have seen, observers in the 1880's had strong doubts of the same character; and even at the end of the First World

[20a] For a fuller analysis see *Capital Expansion, Employment and Economic Stability*, pp. 169-93.

War few could foresee the full influence of such developing industries as the automobile, electric power, and radio communication.

At the present time there are more potential developments of great significance on the industrial horizon than were discernible at the end of the last war. Mention need be made only of synthetic fibres and textiles, plastics, television, electronics, glass, pre-fabricated houses, and air transportation. Many regard the airplane as one of the greatest revolutionary forces in the whole history of industrial development.

The full realization of the constructive possibilities will of course depend upon the restoration of political and economic stability in the world at large, and the elimination of numerous sources of economic maladjustment and confusion within the United States.

In concluding this discussion, it should be noted that the idea that we have reached a stage of arrested development has apparently now been abandoned by its leading advocate. In 1942 Mr. Hansen is quoted as saying:

There is no evidence that our economy is in any sense becoming decadent, inefficient, incapable of continued progress in productivity.[21]

[21] *Chicago Journal of Commerce,* Aug. 31, 1942.

The Phenomenon of "Excess Savings"

The phenomenon of money savings in excess of investment outlets is related in one way to the mature economy conception. If, because of the disappearance of frontiers and an arrested rate of population growth, further private capital expansion were impossible, then obviously we would have no private investment outlets for the current money savings of the people. But independently of a mature economy, it might still be possible that the volume of current money savings had become greater than could be absorbed in productive capital investment. It is contended that the evidence supports the thesis that henceforth money savings are always likely to exceed productive outlets in private enterprise; hence public flotations must fill the breach.

The fact that we had "excess money savings" in the United States in the decade of the twenties was established by the present writer. It was shown that the volume of money savings available for investment was increasing faster than the volume of new securities floated for purposes of productive capital expansion. The primary explanation of this phenomenon was found in the high concentration of national income then existing, which resulted in an increase of money savings relatively to consumptive expenditures. The failure of business enterprise to absorb all of the money savings available was attributed to the lack of adequate consumer demands for the potential output of the new capital. The fact was that existing productive capital was not being fully used.[22]

It was pointed out that there were several possible means whereby the concentration of national income might be lessened, thereby increasing the proportion of the income that would be directed to consumptive channels. These included more steeply progressive income taxes, increased wages, profit sharing, and price reductions—the latter being favored in principle because it brings about the broadest and quickest diffusion of the benefits of technical progress.[23]

The income distribution and savings pattern of the twenties no longer exists. During the decade of the thirties we had in this country a veritable revolution in the distribution of national income. The lowest income groups, both urban and rural, have been assisted by relief payments of various

[22] See *The Formation of Capital*, The Brookings Institution, (1935), Chap. 10.

[23] See *Income and Economic Progress*, The Brookings Institution (1935).

kinds. Farmers have been subsidized, wage rates
have been progressively increased, and a program
of social security and old age benefits has been
established. At the upper level, profits have declined somewhat, and salary and bonus payments
have been appreciably restricted. In consequence
of these developments both the aggregate volume
of money savings and the percentage of the national income directed to savings channels have
been materially reduced. Department of Commerce figures show a decrease in the ratio of private savings to national income from about 12 per
cent in 1929 to an average of roughly 7.5 per cent
in the four-year period 1936-39.[23a]

It is contended by Mr. Hansen that the social
program of the last decade has had little, if any,
effect on the supply of money savings. He argues
that the "consumption function" shows a remark-
able stability and that it is not easy to achieve a
high consumption economy, except by very slow
adjustments. He admits that national policies such
as the redistribution of income, through the tax
machinery and otherwise, work in that direction;
but he concludes that "we have to recognize that
we are dealing here with a function that is highly

[23a] *Survey of Current Business*, May 1942, p. 12.

stable and is not easily changed." He cites as
evidence that in the late twenties consumption
equalled about 88 per cent of the national income
and that in the late thirties it was still 88 per cent.[24]
The implication is that the remaining 12 per cent
in each case represented funds available for private
investment.

But the method employed to prove the case
leaves the vital factor out of the picture. A comparison of *consumption* with *total income* takes no
account of the increases in income and certain
other forms of taxes. With the method employed no
matter how great the increase in taxes, the percentage of national income set aside for private
savings would not change appreciably. To illus-
trate by an extreme example: if we had a national
income of 100 billions with 88 billions of consumption and no taxes, the amount available for private
investment would be 12 billions. If later we had a
national income of 100 billions with 88 billions of
consumption and 12 billions of direct taxes, there
would be *no* money available for private investment. Yet the ratio of consumption to total national
income would still be 88 per cent.

As indicated in the second paragraph preced-

[24] *Fiscal Policy and Business Cycles,* pp. 247-49.

ing, the proportion of the national income saved
dropped from 12 per cent in 1929 to about 7.5 per
cent in the late thirties. The difference is accounted
for chiefly by the increased taxes—which fell
largely upon the groups which normally save most.
The aggregate volume of money savings in the late
thirties was scarcely half that of the twenties.

It remains to be noted, however, that notwithstanding the decrease in the ratio of money savings
to national income, private investment outlets in
the late thirties were still inadequate to absorb all
current money savings. The continuing maladjustment is a reflection not of an exceptional volume
of investment money but rather of a very restricted
amount of new capital flotations. If we had a re-
sumption of anything like the former rate of long-
term capital expansion, the excess of current
money savings as compared with new security flotations would quickly diminish.

It does not appear probable, however, that, in a
new period of business expansion, we shall have a
serious deficiency of money savings. That is, the
proportion of the income that is directed to savings
channels, according to past experience rapidly increases as the level of national income rises. It is
even possible that we might again reach a situation

in which the volume of savings would be in excess
of private investment outlets. The outcome will depend upon the breadth of the distribution of currently produced income, the nature of the tax system, and the degree of confidence in the future of
private enterprise.

Corporate Independence of Capital Markets

The investigations of the Temporary National
Economic Committee endeavored to show that in
recent times business corporations have largely
freed themselves from the necessity of raising
funds in the financial markets, the bulk of the investment funds required now being obtained from
their own internal resources. Accordingly, even if
private business enterprise were reasonably thriv-
ing, it would still be necessary for the government
to provide outlets for current money savings of the
people through continuing flotations of government bonds. This conclusion has been widely accepted in government circles. The contention has
been strikingly stated by Thomas C. Blaisdell, Jr.,
who was chief of the monopoly study of the Securities and Exchange Commission and is now Assistant Director of the National Resources Planning
Board, as follows:

The commonly accepted notion that business enterprises *expand* plant and equipment by obtaining savings through the securities market is greatly exag-
gerated. Business enterprises rely upon the securities
markets, that is, upon the savings of individuals, for
only a small part of *new funds* which they *invest* in
plant and equipment and their going businesses. . . .
If these corporations do not get their funds for expansion from the public financial markets, where do
they get them? Primarily from earnings, that is, from
undistributed profits, depreciation, and depletion.[25]

Evidence submitted by a number of witnesses
before the Temporary National Economic Committee emphasizes that whereas approximately 18
per cent of the gross expenditures for plant and
equipment in the period 1925-29 were financed
from new capital offerings, only about 8 per cent
were thus financed in 1936-37. From this the following conclusion was drawn:

It is evident that business enterprises rely relatively
little upon the capital market for their investment
funds. . . . Moreover, there is reason to believe that
the role of the capital market is declining in terms
of a long-run trend. It is true that we do not as yet
have an adequate statistical basis for the calculation

[25] Italics supplied. Address before the Institute of Public
Affairs, University of Virginia, July 10, 1939. See also Marriner
S. Eccles, " 'Government Securities Outlook' Conference,"
Savings Bank Journal, March 1940.

of a long-run trend in view of the incomplete recoveries of 1936-37 and 1939-40.[26]

The conclusion drawn from the data presented is entirely misleading. *Gross* capital expenditures include outlays for maintenance and replacement as well as for new plant and equipment. It is an elementary principle of accounting and of business operation that the replacement of depreciating or wasting assets *should* be provided from internal depreciation and depletion allowances rather than out of undistributed earnings or from new capital flotations. Combining outlays for replacement with those for expansion simply obscures the question under consideration. With this method the corresponding figures for any decade would show that a relatively small percentage of gross capital expenditures (for maintenance and replacement as well as expansion) was obtained from the general capital market. This is because outlays for maintenance and replacement of existing plant and equipment are always large. And in any period of depression, when new capital outlays are subnormal, expenditures for maintenance and replacement of existing plant and equipment would naturally constitute the bulk of the total.

[26] Hansen, *Fiscal Policy and Business Cycles*, p. 386.

In his testimony before the Temporary National Economic Committee Mr. Hansen calls attention to the fact that gross capital expenditures do include outlays for maintenance and replacement, and that capital *expansion* is the real problem in which we are interested. But he nevertheless applies the term *investment* to gross capital outlays and not merely to *new* plant and equipment. Moreover, he definitely implies that the decline in the thirties in the percentage of gross capital expenditures financed in the capital market suggests that the role of the capital market may be declining.

It may possibly be that dependence upon the capital market for expansion money is decreasing—that an ever-larger proportion is being obtained from undistributed earnings; but there is no evidence to support this conclusion. Since available figures do not show expenditures for maintenance and replacement separately from those for expansion, one cannot know whether business was more or less dependent upon the capital market for expansion funds than was the case in the twenties.[27]

[27] It should be noted here that capital replacements may, because of the greater efficiency of the new units, yield an increase in productive output. We may therefore have a continuous expansion in productivity without any increase in total capital investment. But it would still be necessary to use individual savings or undistributed earnings in constructing

In considering this problem it should be remembered that a substantial part of American business expansion has always been financed from undistributed earnings. In his book on *Fiscal Policy and Business Cycles,* Mr. Hansen devotes a chapter to early financing methods, and concludes that in the case of both individual and corporate business

> . . . Most of the great fortunes started with small savings, together with small support from friends of meager means. Profits were plowed back into the business and expansion came from internal growth.
> Other examples of less spectacular individual fortunes, of business corporations springing from meager individual savings, and of small beginnings with growth financed mainly from reinvested profits, fill the pages of American business annals throughout the nineteenth century and even down to the present day.[28]

While this evidence may not be conclusive, it certainly does not support the contention "that the role of the capital market is declining in terms of a long-run trend."

---

additional increments of capital. Only provided the depreciation reserves are greater than the actual depreciation can expansion money be obtained from this source. Because of the increasingly careful scrutiny of depreciation items by the Treasury, it is highly probable that depreciation reserves as a source of capital expansion are much less important now than formerly.

[28] Pp. 376, 379.

The truth is that we do not know for sure whether business as a whole will be less dependent upon the capital markets in the future than it has been in the past. It will depend upon factors which cannot now be fully gauged. That war developments have changed the picture somewhat is apparent from the fact that some of our largest corporations have arranged for large credit accommodations extending over a period of years.

The 1937 Episode

It has already been noted that the depression of 1937 played an important part in the evolution of the doctrine that continuous or expanding deficits are essential to prosperity—that any reduction in net government outlays will only lead to disaster. In testifying before the Temporary National Economic Committee Mr. Hansen said:

I think that recession of '37 was to a very large extent due to just that decline in the net income-creating expenditures of the Government.[29]

The implication of the phrase *net income-creating expenditures* in lieu of *treasury deficit* will be observed. It should be noted, however, that the decline in *net income-creating expenditures* was

[29] Hearings, Pt. 9, p. 3553.

not due to an actual decrease in treasury outlays; it was rather the result of the increased tax receipts which naturally accompanied the prosperity period.[30] This automatic increase in tax receipts is evidently looked upon as more or less equivalent to a *positive* curtailment of government financing and a corresponding restriction of purchasing power. It would appear that we must expand government expenditures at least in proportion to increases in tax receipts, lest the shrinking cash deficit —that is, the decline in income-creating expenditures—dry up the stream of purchasing power.

This analysis obviously overlooks the fact that it is *aggregate* national purchasing power, *private and public,* that counts. The statistics of income disbursements, public and private, show that aggregate purchasing power was rising rapidly during the period in question.

The evolution of Mr. Hansen's thinking is indicated by the following statement which was made only a few months before the one quoted above. Speaking of fiscal policy as a means of restricting

[30] Apart from the bulge in expenditures resulting from the soldier bonus payments of the early summer of 1936, the level of expenditures was rising. The outgo for the first five months of the calendar year 1937 aggregated 3,079 million dollars as compared with 2,740 millions in the same months of 1936.

the fluctuations of the business cycle he said:

> As the national income . . . approaches 70 billion dollars I suggest that the net income-creating governmental expenditures ought to be tapered off. As we approach this income level, the economic situation becomes increasingly explosive. . . . We encounter the familiar vicious spiral of rising costs and rising prices with growing inefficiency.[31]

According to the later philosophy a decrease in "net income-creating expenditures"—whether as a result of increased tax receipts or reduced Treasury expenditures—can only result in depression.

In summary, the view that we have reached a stage of economic development in which continuous deficit financing is necessary, is not sustained by the evidence and analysis that have been submitted.

(1) The mature economy assumption is not supported by the evidence; and it has apparently now been abandoned by its leading exponent.

(2) The argument that we are confronted with a permanent excess of money savings is based upon a fallacious comparison—that of consumption with national income—which takes no account of increasing taxes and their effect upon savings.

---

[31] "Economic Progress and Declining Population Growth," *The American Economic Review*, March 1939, p. 14.

(3) The belief that business corporations have in recent years largely freed themselves from dependence on the general capital market grows out of a failure to differentiate between the replacement of old and the creation of new plant and equipment.

(4) The contention that the depression of 1937 was due to a reduction in the government's "net contributions to purchasing power" belies the pump priming theory itself; and it overlooks the significant fact that *aggregate* purchasing power—public and private combined—was rapidly increasing up to the time the depression began.

2. New Credit Agencies to Finance the Future

Proceeding from the assumption that the private capital credit mechanism has permanently broken down, Mr. Adolf A. Berle, Jr., suggests a way out of the dilemma of modern capitalism through the medium of a new type of capital credit bank. As already noted, these credit banks, deriving funds from Federal Reserve credit extensions, would make loans for public capital enterprises, virtually without interest. The reach of this conception is indicated by the following statement:

If wealth is to be created by creation of government

debt, the scope of government enterprise must be largely increased. Briefly, the government will have to enter into the direct financing of activities now supposed to be private; and a continuance of that direct financing must be inevitably that the government ultimately will control and own those activities. . . . Over a period of years, the government will gradually come to own most of the productive plants of the United States.

This is certainly so fundamentally a change in the course of American life that the decision to make it should be taken for reasons other than relief of a series of temporary difficulties. If the country desires to make wealth creation a function of government (I personally believe it must do so in larger measure than it has heretofore) the choice should be the considered choice of the country, and not the result of a policy of drift.[32]

For the conception of these government credit banks Mr. Berle has expressed his indebtedness to the present writer. In a series of articles on Commercial Banking and Capital Formation written in 1918[33] I had shown—among other things—that bank credit expansion, contrary to the belief of the classical economists, had played a constructive or creative role in economic development. In brief,

[32] Hearings before the Temporary National Economic Committee, Pt. 9, p. 4069.
[33] See *Journal of Political Economy*, May, June, July, and November, 1918.

the credit currency created by the banking system provided funds with which to construct new capital without waiting for the accumulation of money savings. It was demonstrated that bank credit was, in fact, extensively employed in financing long-term capital development and that the tempo of economic expansion had thus been accelerated.[34]

In his testimony before the Temporary National Economic Committee, Mr. Berle referred at some length to these articles, stating:

I do not think that the revolutionary quality of this discovery has been adequately appreciated. If true, it meant that our ideas on the whole subject of capital and capital credit had to change. . . . Moulton's study pointed to a definite reorganization of the banking structure. It at least suggested the possibility that long-term investment might be assisted or carried on through properly controlled banking operations.

The only relevancy of these articles to Mr. Berle's proposal is in connection with the conception of bank credit as a creative force. But he has here missed the fact of crucial significance. When bank credit was created for the financing of

---

[34] Since increased production accompanied the process, the result of the credit expansion was not merely to raise prices. Incidentally, the analysis revealed that the financing of long-term investment by means of bank loans did not destroy the liquidity of the banking system.

private capital expansion, it was always expected
that the loans would be repaid out of the earnings
made possible by the new plant and equipment;
and, in the vast majority of cases, such loans were
in due course liquidated. The fact that new loans
were usually being made faster than old ones were
being liquidated and that total outstanding loans
were thus expanding did not, of course, alter the
fact that each and every loan was made on business principles and paid for out of the earnings
resulting from the creation of new capital.

That this fundamental point is overlooked by
Mr. Berle is evident from the fact that his new
capital credit banks are not designed to make loans
merely or mainly for self-liquidating enterprises.
The loans would also be made—at nominal interest
rates—for a wide range of public purposes conceived as useful to society but without regard to
their revenue-producing possibilities. In principle,
he apparently sees no reason why one need be
concerned about repayment.

Further light is thrown on Mr. Berle's conception of financial problems by the way in which
he relates my analysis of commercial banking operations to the evolution of the new philosophy of
public finance. He says that the articles mentioned,
long ignored by American economists, were even-

tually discovered by the Swedes; that Dr. Hjalmar Schacht imported the idea from Sweden and made it the basis of the Reich's new fiscal policy, and that we in turn learned from Germany the potentialities of public credit in expanding production and employment.[35]

It is true that the articles in question were extensively reviewed by Swedish and other Scandinavian economists. But if Schacht imported his financial plan from Sweden, the essence was lost in transit, for Germany's financing methods have little if any relationship to the thesis of the articles. Although Mr. Berle evidently thinks American methods of financing the present war are based on a Nazi model, the fact is that they do not differ essentially from those followed since 1933, or from those used in the First World War.

3. Public Debt as Support for the Banks

According to the new conception, a very important service rendered by an expanding public debt is to support the commercial banks and other financial institutions. Their large holdings of government securities (for data see page 59) reveal the importance of the government's service.

[35] In an address at The Brookings Institution, 1940.

The banks . . . perform a necessary public service and they must be supported somehow. If they did not receive the interest on the bonds they hold they might be compelled to increase their service charges or to lower the interest they pay on deposits, or both; indeed a great many of them have recently increased their service charges, not to mention lowering their interest allowances, claiming that their receipts would not be sufficient otherwise to support them. The same principle holds with respect to the government trust funds and the life insurance companies; they must have the revenue from interest receipts or obtain the funds from the public in other ways.[36]

This argument might be greatly extended. It could be contended that railroads and public utilities and manufacturing corporations (which are large owners of government bonds) also serve the public. They have to be supported somehow, and, if they are not supported by the government through interest payments, they might have to raise rates or prices charged the public. The idea that it is the government which supports the public is in sharp contrast to the former conception that it is the public which supports the government. The new idea obviously ignores the tax side of public finance.

It has hitherto been assumed that private cor-

[36] *Fortune*, November 1942, p. 170.

porations of every type *should* charge the public sufficiently to cover the costs involved, and to permit the making of profits and also the payment of taxes for the general support of government. Traditionally, banks have not been singled out as deserving of government subsidy on the ground that they alone serve the public. In any case, the primary service of commercial banks is to business enterprises, and thus their service to the public which Mr. Hansen stresses is chiefly through the services which business enterprises render the public.

4. Is the Public Debt a Real Debt?

The proponents of the philosophy that the only hope for full employment and continuing prosperity lies in permanent deficit financing recognize, of course, that this means a continuous expansion of the public debt. The economic implications of an ever-expanding public debt are, moreover, given consideration. We are advised that an internal public debt is not a menace and that we should not be "intimidated" by it. "On the contrary, instead of looking upon [it] with the sort of awe that was inspired in our savage ancestors by some incomprehensible phenomenon such as lightning, we must take a leaf out of the book of modern science. . . . It is, in fact, so different from what we commonly think of as debt . . . that it should scarcely be called debt at all." An internal public debt "has none of the essential earmarks of a private debt."[37]

As a preliminary, it is desirable to clear up some possible sources of confusion or misunderstanding about the public debt problem. In this way the range of controversy or disagreement will be narrowed and the basic issues more clearly revealed.

Must the Budget Always be in Balance?

The answer to this question is obviously *no*. The question is raised here only because it is frequently implied that those who are concerned about perpetual increase of the debt are adherents of "the obsolete conception" of a *permanently balanced budget*. It is of course generally conceded that in times of war public expenditures may have to run ahead of current tax receipts. Moreover, nearly all students of public finance are, I believe, in agreement that in times of depression and readjustment, public outlays not covered by taxes may be both essential and helpful in stimulating recovery. As

[37] The same, p. 166.

for prosperity periods, it has always been taken for granted that the budget should provide a surplus with which to reduce public debt. In so far as there may be disagreement with respect to the use of public expenditures in conjunction with alternating periods of depression and prosperity (the so-called "compensatory fiscal action") it would relate only to the degree to which fiscal policy, as distinguished from other types of policy, might advisedly be relied upon to promote recovery.

Must the Public Debt be Paid Off?

It is widely believed that a public debt created by a war or other national emergency must, or at least should, in due course be completely liquidated. This view is fostered by official statements such as those quoted on pages 2 and 3. Students of public finance are, however, agreed on the proposition that there is no necessity of reducing a public debt to zero. Many countries have had large public debts for a century or more. Even the United States government has not been completely out of debt since 1835. While the large debt incurred during the Civil War might readily have been extinguished in a generation, it was decided that some public debt was desirable—as security for bank note issues and as a highly conservative investment. The debt of the First World War was reduced during the twenties from approximately 26 billions to 16 billions; but no one seriously argued that it was necessary or desirable that the debt be completely paid off.

It is only necessary that the debt be kept under easy control—that is, well within revenue possibilities. Fiscal experts have always regarded it as wise to reduce the debt materially in easy times in order to have a margin of safety for possible hard times in the future. This is simply common sense, prudent financial management.

Under What Conditions May a Public Debt Be Gradually Expanded?

There are two circumstances under which a gradual expansion of the public debt might occur without endangering financial stability. First, if the government floats bonds for the purpose of constructing a public enterprise which yields sufficient revenues to cover maintenance, operation, and replacement costs, together with interest on the government's investment, the accompanying expansion of the debt need cause no concern. The bonds issued for the construction of the Panama

Canal are an illustration. The situation here is analogous to the common practice of private corporations in floating bonds with which to construct revenue-producing plant and equipment.

Second, at a time when, in consequence of private business expansion, the national income is steadily rising, with the tax-paying capacity likewise increasing, a country would obviously be able to support an increasing public debt. But prudent management, with forethought for possible difficulties in the future, still would suggest the importance of restraining the debt in order to provide an ample margin of safety for future periods of adversity.

How Does an Internal Debt Differ from a Foreign Debt?

It has long been recognized and repeatedly pointed out that there is an essential difference between a domestic public debt and an external public debt. In the case of a foreign debt the revenues collected from American taxpayers with which to pay interest have to be transferred to bondholders living in another country. In final analysis this means that we have to export goods and services to foreigners in order to obtain the foreign cur-

rency required. In the case of an internal debt the
interest is paid to bondholders living in the same
country as the taxpayers; hence exports and the
acquisition of foreign currency are not involved.
This obvious difference does not, however, dispose
of the issue whether an internal public debt is of
any economic significance.

With these preliminary questions cleared, we
are in a position to consider the arguments advanced in support of the conclusion that a domestic
debt involves no dangers but has positive advan-
tages. It will be necessary to scrutinize a number
of specific contentions.

The argument that an internal public debt bears no resemblance to a private debt

The view that "a public debt has none of the
earmarks of a private debt," and that "it should
scarcely be called a debt at all" arises from con-
templation of the fact that the money collected as
taxes flows back to the people as interest receipts.
"Taxes will be collected to service the bonds, and
when interest or principal payments are made on
them the money is merely shifted about within the
economic system."

The same line of reasoning might be applied to the debt of a state or a city, if such debt were held wholly by the citizens of the particular state or municipality. And, if we consider our states and our cities as a collective whole, all state and local public indebtedness could be looked upon as not really debt at all. Moreover, if we view the corporations of the country collectively, their bonded indebtedness would not really be debt because the income collected from the American people for the services rendered is paid out to the American people as interest. In this way we get rid of all debt problems.

On second thought, however, it will be reflected that *particular* railroad companies or industrial corporations, or state or local governments, might find themselves in difficulty because they are unable to make financial ends meet. Likewise, one may reflect that the federal government might, under certain circumstances, find it impossible to collect sufficient revenues to meet its interest and other obligations. National governments have, in fact, frequently found themselves in serious financial difficulties. Thus the mere fact that in all cases the collection of revenues and the payment of interest "merely shifts money around within the economic system" has not, as historical evidence shows, eliminated the debt problem.

While Mr. Hansen argues in some places that a public debt has none of the earmarks of a private debt, elsewhere he makes them directly analogous. For example:

> . . . Public debt might be likened to the capital account of a corporation, made up, say, of long-term mortgage bonds and of one or more classes of stock. Such liabilities, it is important to remember, are offset by assets on the other side of the balance sheet. So long as these are of a character to produce sufficient earnings to meet the capital charges, including dividends on the stock, nobody would ever think of the corporation as being over capitalized. The essential element determining the soundness of the concern is the *ratio* of its earning power to its capital account. . . . Precisely the same principle holds with respect to the public debt of a nation, of which the source of earnings or revenue is usually taxation. If the power to raise revenue is in manageable ratio to the capital charges (debt service), it is proper to say that the nation is not, so to speak, over capitalized.[38]

From this statement one could hardly conclude that public debts are something wholly different from other types of indebtedness.

[38] *Fortune,* November 1942, p. 169.

The contention that tax payments and interest receipts are in fairly close adjustment

The contention that a domestic public debt has little significance because the income is merely shifted about within the economic system, going out of one pocket into another, was extensively discussed after the last war. At that time the basic issue was stated by the present writer as follows:

It is undoubtedly true that the interest on the domestic debt accrues to the people of any given country in the form of revenue. But the particular individuals who pay the taxes do not usually receive back in interest anything like the precise amount of funds that they have parted with in the form of taxes. Some receive a great deal more from the government than they pay to the government; others receive a great deal less. The process thus involves a wholesale redistribution of wealth.[39]

That the process might at times involve a considerable redistribution of wealth is admitted by Mr. Hansen. He stated the matter as follows in 1941:

In so far as the government can borrow from small savers, an increase in the public debt will not prove unfavorable to an equitable distribution of wealth.

[39] John F. Bass and Harold G. Moulton, *America and the Balance Sheet of Europe*, p. 61.

But if the growth in the public debt is very rapid, it will not be possible for relatively small savers to take any large proportion of the new securities issued. They will be absorbed by the rich and the well to do, and by large corporations. A rapid growth in the public debt is, therefore, likely to intensify the inequality in wealth distribution.[40]

But in 1942—a year of extraordinarily rapid debt increase, in which the bulk of the bond purchases were made by individuals of large means and by the commercial banks—Mr. Hansen contends that "under modern conditions" the ideal of an identity between individual tax payments and individual interest receipts is

more closely approximated than was formerly the case. Most of the debt is now actually very widely distributed among individual citizens or among institutions that serve the citizens; and this state of affairs may be expected to continue.[41]

He cites as evidence the following distribution of government bond holdings as of June 30, 1942, and adds that

Only a little reflection is needed to see that every one of these groups of bondholders—except the "others"—does in fact serve the public or is itself the public; and even the "others" are made up in con-

[40] *Fiscal Policy and Business Cycles*, p. 179.
[41] *Fortune*, November 1942, p. 170.

siderable measure of endowments, foundations, and trust funds, rather than rich individuals.[42]

	Billions	Per cent
Commercial banks	$28.8	37.7
Life insurance companies and mutual savings banks	12.9	16.8
Purchasers of savings bonds	13.1	17.1
Government trust funds	10.6	13.8
Others	11.2	14.6

The obvious intent here is to convey the impression that these figures show an extremely wide distribution of bond holdings among the masses—that they are not held mainly by the rich. The data cited do not, however, throw any light on the breadth of the distribution of government bonds. The purchasers of savings bonds include wealthy individuals and business corporations as well as individuals of small means, and the mere statement that there are 13.1 billions outstanding does not show who holds them.

Nearly 40 per cent of government issues are held by commercial banks, and the proportion is rapidly rising. The bulk of deposits of the commercial banks are those made by large corporations, and represent working capital funds. At the end of 1942 the average size of the commercial deposits (ex-

[42] The same.

cluding government and bank deposits) of five large New York banks, having aggregate deposits of five billion dollars, was roughly $30,000. Quantitatively speaking, the bulk of the deposits of most small commercial banks also are those of business enterprises or of individuals of substantial means.

Even if it could be shown that government bond holdings were now very widely distributed, it would still be necessary to show that the tax burden is distributed similarly. But no evidence on this point is submitted.

The argument that "costs and income are just opposite sides of the same shield"

It is emphasized that "Every cent expended, public or private, becomes income for the members of our own society." This conception apparently explains the statement of the National Resources Planning Board that costs are of no significance, that "doing the job pays the bill."[43] Since the receipts are necessarily identical with the disbursements everything is satisfactory: cost equals income; and income equals cost.

Note that this argument is applied not only to interest on the public debt, but to *all* public ex-

[43] See p. 4.

penditures. Veterans' compensation does not really cost us anything because the veterans receive the income. The war does not cost us anything because every cent expended (within the country) is income to the American people. Note also that the statement includes private as well as public expenditures. Since the costs of private business are represented on the opposite side of the shield by income disbursements, no one need worry about costs.

The initial error in this proposition is that costs and income are *not* opposite sides of the *same* shield. The *costs* are costs to the Treasury; the *income* is income to the public. And the Treasury cannot get back all of its outlays in the form of taxes. Hence there is no identity between outflow and inflow. The Treasury goes into debt.

The second error embodies the basic fallacy in the new philosophy of public expenditure and debt. The argument that all government expenditures, for whatever purpose, generate money income and thereby provide the means for liquidating the costs fails to take account of the differing effects of varying types of public expenditure upon *future income*.

When a government constructs a capital enterprise which sells goods or services in the market it derives *revenues*—presumably sufficient to cover operating costs and interest, to provide for eventual replacement, and to yield an income to the government. Such a public outlay would impose no additional tax burden on the rest of the community. The enterprise is not only self-supporting but may even help support the government over a period of years.

Non-revenue-producing public works cannot cover their operating, maintenance and replacement costs, or interest charges. Hence they involve continuing costs which must be borne by the taxpayers. It is obvious that most types of public works are useful or enjoyable; but it remains true that they do not for that reason yield continuing revenues with which to carry their costs. From a *fiscal* point of view, instead of carrying themselves, and possibly yielding net revenues to the government in the future, they involve continuing annual outlays for an indefinite period. Similarly, expenditures for veterans' compensation, doles, interest, and so forth—necessary though they may be— provide no continuing source of public revenues.

But it is contended by Mr. Hansen that all the free services provided by the government can readily be made to take care of themselves by the simple process of expanding the nation's money supply and hence its taxable capacity.

"When the government provides free services, some appropriate monetary expansion is justified. This would permit the collection of taxes sufficient to cover the expenses of operation together with amortization and interest charges."[44]

This seems to say that if: first, we expend public money to construct non-revenue-producing public works, to support the unemployed, and so forth; and then, second, issue an additional volume of money, the taxes will rise sufficiently to liquidate all the costs involved. By what process and to whom the additional money (from which the additional taxes would be derived) is to be issued is not made clear. Nor is there apparently any recognition of the fact that, in order to carry the *continuing* costs involved, this *additional* income would have to be issued not once only but in *each succeeding* year. The basic error in thinking pointed out above still remains. The Treasury simply cannot get back in taxes, levied upon the additional income it distributes through its disbursements, as much money as it pays out.

[44] *Fiscal Policy and Business Cycles,* p. 170.

This general problem may be illustrated by war-time expenditures. Such outlays exert, *immediately speaking*, quite as powerful an economic stimulus, provide as much employment, and generate as much current money income as any other kind of expenditures, public or private. But neither the munitions and supplies consumed by the military establishment, nor the fixed capital embedded in bomber and fighter planes, in government shipyards and docks, in naval bases and naval vessels, or in military roads and army fortifications yield tax revenues. Moreover, they cannot carry their own operating costs or provide for their own replacement. They simply represent dead-weight charges against the rest of the economic system. In addition to their original costs, they will entail large annual charges for continued upkeep.

That public expenditures for war purposes do not generate a sufficient increase in income to bring the budget more nearly into balance is readily apparent. When the government expends 20 billion dollars for war purposes the 20 billions of national income thus generated is only in small part available as revenue to the Treasury. If, say, 20 per cent of the increased income be collected in taxes, the government would receive back as a result of this operation only 4 billions, with a resulting increase of 16 billions in the public debt. This is what has been happening since 1940. This is what will continue to happen with non-revenue-producing government outlays.

By way of contrast, it is well to note what happens when national income increases as a result of private business expansion. Then the ensuing increase in tax receipts is clear gain for the Treasury. Instead of an increasing deficit we get, inevitably, a decreasing deficit.

It must also be noted that an ever-expanding public debt would adversely affect the level of national income in the future by checking investment. The accompanying increase in taxes and the fears of more to come could hardly fail to prove a serious deterrent to new investment. Hence the rate of capital expansion and the rise in national income would be retarded.

5. Limits to the Public Debt

Notwithstanding the contention that the public debt is not a real debt and that we can be at ease because there is merely involved a shifting about of money income, Mr. Hansen has come to have some reservations with respect to the ultimate size of the public debt. In a recent article—although he still argues most of the time that the growth of the public debt is of no real significance—he finally reaches the surprising conclusion that "the debt should cause no anxiety so long as it is kept within safe limits."[44a]

An attempt is made, moreover, to provide an index for determining when the debt is approaching the danger point. He says that the limits of safety will depend upon a number of factors, such as the level of national income, the kind of taxation levied, and the wisdom of the public investment and public expenditures made. "But the all-important factor is the level—the sustained level—of the national income."

He suggests that the debt might safely be double the national income. This conclusion is based upon the alleged fact that on two occasions the British debt has been twice the size of the British national income—in the years 1818 and 1923 respectively.[45] British statisticians are in agreement, however, that there are no reliable income estimates for the British Isles prior to 1860. The 1818 figure is a mere guess, ventured by a member of the House

[44a] *Fortune*, November 1942, p. 175.
[45] *Fiscal Policy and Business Cycles*, p. 136.

of Commons.[46] Nor does the 1923 figure cited by Mr. Hansen prove that Britain could support a debt twice the size of the national income. In the quotation given above, he emphasizes a *sustained level* of income in relation to debt. The fact is that the high debt ratio in 1923 was merely the result of the shrinkage of income during a period of acute depression. It was a temporary phenomenon, nothing more.

Moreover, the safe limits of public debt cannot be gauged by comparing the national income with the public debt alone. In addition to interest charges, account must be taken of military outlays, pensions, relief and social security payments, and the level of ordinary operating expenses. The lower these types of outlays, the higher might be the ratio of debt to national income; and vice versa. In 1923 the British government was not carrying a fiscal load for military, social, and other purposes comparable to that which will doubtless be involved in the future. Viewing the debt problem in isolation, without considering the magnitude of other probable fiscal requirements, furnishes no guidance as to the safe limits of debt expansion.

[46] Speech by Mr. Curwen, Mar. 7, 1821. See Hansard, Vol. 4, p. 1147.

Mr. Hansen concludes the discussion of the safe limits of public debt expansion as follows:

There is little reason to fear that, with the sort of fiscal management we shall have a right to expect, the debt could not safely go well beyond double the national income if necessary. Certainly we have no occasion to think of the debt limit as being like the edge of a precipice from which we must always stay carefully away.[47]

Thus while he is evidently not prepared to say whether the debt should be permitted to reach two, two and a half, or even three times the national income, he feels sure that the kind of fiscal experts we shall have a right to expect in the future will know the answer and be prepared to impose the necessary restraints.

The ideas and figures that are being played with these days with respect to "the public debt potential" may be illustrated by reference to a recent contribution[48] of Seymour E. Harris, Associate Professor of Economics at Harvard University, now on leave with the Office of Price Administration. Mr. Harris suggests that

[47] *Fortune*, November 1942, p. 175.
[48] In *Postwar Economic Problems*, February 1943, edited by Seymour E. Harris, Chap. 10.

In one sense, there is no limit to the growth of public debt, for, as debt charges rise, the taxation of holders of this debt may rise at an equal rate.

This means that a debt of any size can be handled by the simple process of imposing a tax of 100 per cent on the interest received by bondholders. The government would thus collect back from the bondholders the precise amounts which had been paid to them. Mr. Harris neglects to point out that a 100 per cent tax on interest would in effect be a repudiation of the interest obligation, and that under such circumstances the government would find no voluntary market for subsequent issues.

But in illustrating concretely the extent to which the debt might possibly rise, Mr. Harris does not go so far as to assume that *all* of the debt burden should be assessed against the bondholders. He suggests that only 60 per cent might come from this source, the balance being derived from taxes on other incomes. Thus instead of having a 2½ per cent security, each bondholder would have in effect a 1 per cent bond—with market values affected accordingly. Passing by the question of justice to the purchasers of government securities, Mr. Harris says that

If, in a period of fifty years, we could attain a national income of $200 billion, plus the interest on government securities, then a public debt of $4000 billion [4 trillion] might well be within the realm of possibility.

Assuming an interest rate of 2½ per cent, the interest would amount to 100 billion dollars annually. According to Mr. Harris' scheme of assessing the burdens, 60 per cent of the interest on the public debt would be taken out of the hides of government bondholders; the balance, or 40 billions, would be assessed equally against wages, salaries, and farm incomes, on the one hand, and dividends and profits on the other.

This would involve the following tax rates to meet the debt charges alone: On government bondholders, 60 per cent; on capitalists, 33⅓ per cent; on wages, salaries, and farm income, 14 per cent. In addition, it would still be necessary to raise taxes sufficient to meet all of the other expenditures of the federal government, which Mr. Harris estimates might be at least 35 to 40 billion dollars. In addition, still, would be the taxes necessary to support state and local governments.

In short, Mr. Harris would have us believe that, if the national income were gradually increased from 100 to 200 billions (not counting government interest disbursements), we could perhaps support a public debt twenty times as large as the estimated debt at the end of the fiscal year 1944. In any event, he concludes: "the man in the street worries too much over a public debt of $100 to $200 billion."

6. The Role of Taxation

The implications of the new philosophy of public debt from the point of view of taxation are engaging. If the growth of the public debt is of no moment, one might at first thought be inclined to ask—Why go to all the trouble and expense of collecting taxes? Why burden the public with ever-increasing levies? Indeed, if the purpose of fiscal policy is not to balance the budget but to obtain the largest possible "net income-creating" expenditures—as measured by the size of the cash *deficit* —why not promote the desired end by cancelling all taxes?

That a reorientation of thought with respect to tax policy would be necessary is suggested in a statement already quoted: "Once freed from the obsolete concept of the balanced budget, the larger uses of federal taxes can be creatively ex-

plored."[49] The suggested creative purposes are:
(1) To regulate the distribution of income; and (2)
to prevent inflation in periods of full employment.[50] These objectives, as we shall see, might be
realized on a very low plane of taxation.

Heretofore, the use of the tax machinery to redistribute income has been combined with the
purpose of raising very large amounts of revenue;
hence we have had extremely high taxes on the
rich, moderately high taxes on the well-to-do, and
substantial taxes (direct and indirect) on the lower
income groups. But if the *sole* purpose of taxation
should be to redistribute income this could be accomplished equally well by simply abolishing all
taxes on the masses, retaining only those on the
high income groups. Indeed, even the taxes on the
higher incomes might be eliminated by the use of
more direct methods of leveling incomes, such as
the regulation of profits and salaries. Thus, as far
as the realization of the first objective is concerned,
the volume of taxes might well be negligible.

The second objective, the prevention of inflation
in periods of full employment, might also, *theo-
retically*, be achieved without resort to taxation.

[49] See p. 10.
[50] Hansen, *Fiscal Policy and Business Cycles*, p. 175.

As ordinarily stated, the problem at such times is to mop up excess purchasing power; and this can be done *either* by taxation *or* by the sale of government bonds to the investing public rather than to the banks. In both cases the funds obtained would come from individual incomes, thus reducing the amounts available for consumption expenditures. If, therefore, we were not concerned with the size of the government deficit, there is no reason why we should not eliminate the tax method of absorbing purchasing power—relying entirely on the sale of government bonds to individuals.[51]

As a practical matter, bearing in mind the double objective of redistributing income and controlling inflation, it would, however, still doubtless be found advantageous to make some use of taxation. But if the new philosophy were sound—we could have a very great easing of the burden of taxation. Total tax collections could be enormously reduced and the present complicated tax system with all its administrative difficulties and inequities could be virtually eliminated. All that would be required would be a properly graduated income tax, supplemented, perhaps, by estate taxes.

[51] The issues involved in controlling inflation will be discussed in the ensuing section.

V. THE PUBLIC DEBT AND INFLATION

In the popular mind the public debt is closely related to inflation. How is a great advance in commodity prices to be prevented if the public debt is allowed to increase continuously? Does not history show that an enormous rise in the public debt always results in disastrous inflation? We are assured by the advocates of the new philosophy that inflation can readily be controlled, even though the debt is constantly expanding.

Fiscal management under the new system of public finance, it should be noted, would involve control at two stages: First, whenever we are *not* making full use of our productive resources the Treasury would stimulate further expansion through borrowings from the commercial banks. If the banks should perchance at any time be unwilling to purchase all the government securities offered, the government might possibly endeavor to meet the situation by taking over the banks. Or, as an alternative, the Treasury might turn directly to the Federal Reserve system, which is now under political control. Still another alternative would be for the Treasury to issue its own non-interest-bearing notes.

The second stage is reached when the expansion process has resulted in full use of our productive resources. To check inflation at this point, it is held that the Treasury would henceforth cease to borrow from the banks, and raise the money required solely from taxes or from bonds sold to the investing public. Since the government's revenues would no longer be derived in part from bank credit expansion, the total money supply would no longer increase; and inflation could not occur. Stated in theoretical terms, the problem sounds simple. But, as we shall see, the inflation appears much more complex than the foregoing statement would indicate, and the practical difficulties involved cannot be surmounted without a very elaborate system of control.

1. The Problem of Control

The nature of the inflation control problem thus raised may best be revealed by reference to the situation with which the United States is confronted in the year 1943. We are now operating the bulk of our productive resources at maximum capacity; we not only have full employment but a shortage of manpower. We have, moreover, a huge excess of purchasing power requiring absorption by the Treasury.

Control over prices in this situation is being
sought by two methods, or from two sides. On the
one hand, we are attempting to drain off the excess
purchasing power by means of taxes and bond
sales to the public; and, on the other, we are trying
to prevent further increases in wage rates and in
the prices of farm raw materials from generating
an inflation spiral operating from the cost side.

The control of wage rates and agricultural prices
involves political as well as economic factors.
Group pressures exerted on Congress and the Administration led to substantial increases in wage
rates and farm prices long before the stage of full
employment was reached; and the Office of Price
Administration was not able to prevent a considerable advance in the prices of manufactured products, flowing from the antecedent increases in
wage rates and farm prices. When the stage of full
employment came, the problem of control was
gravely complicated because of the uneven operation of the so-called "vicious spiral," which inevitably resulted in continuing demands from certain groups for further upward adjustments of
prices and wages. Under such circumstances the
stabilization of costs is as much a political as an
economic problem. Consequently, no one can give
assurance that the inflation process, operating from

the cost side, can be checked at the stage of full employment.

On the demand side, the control of excess purchasing power presents quite as great difficulties. When the stage of full employment is reached, is the Treasury in a position to cease borrowing from the commercial banks and to rely exclusively upon taxes and bond sales to the public? Despite the restrictions imposed upon consumption and the powerful patriotic urge to support the government's financial program, the Treasury deems it impossible at the present time to raise by taxes and bond sales to individuals all of the funds required. As a practical matter it is recognized that at least a third of the financial needs will have to be met by the banks. Compulsory payroll withholding taxes might conceivably absorb all of the excess purchasing power currently accruing to wage and salary groups; but such a tax cannot be collected on a current basis from farmers and various professional groups.

It has come to be recognized in every country at war that prices cannot be controlled through fiscal policy alone. Direct control over costs, supplemented by rationing, has been found indispensable. Moreover, increases in costs are directly related to the expansion of purchasing power. In the

United States, for example, the excess purchasing power existing in 1942 could not have been controlled without adequate control over wage rates and farm prices—the principal avenues by which the expanding purchasing power reached the channels of circulation.

The experience of other countries during this war has shown that without controls over primary cost factors, an inflationary cycle cannot be prevented. And it has also been demonstrated that given such controls, and an *effective rationing system,* the rise in commodity prices can be checked even when the fiscal program is not adequate to meet the situation. Canada and England, as well as Germany, kept prices well in hand in 1942, even though all of the excess purchasing power was not currently absorbed.

In time of peace the control of inflation at the stage of full employment would be even more difficult than in time of war. The pressures emanating from special groups would be quite as insistent; and the necessities of a great national emergency could not be invoked as a restraining influence. The sale of bonds to the investing public would be more difficult because opportunities for investment elsewhere would be more abundant and the patriotic urge for assisting the government less compelling. Moreover, at the very time the Treasury was seeking to check inflation, the situation might be complicated by heavy public liquidations of existing bond holdings in order to obtain spending money. This problem may confront the Treasury in the early postwar period.

If one were to assume that as the stage of full employment is reached the budget would be virtually in balance, the problem of control through fiscal policy would seem to present less difficulty. But, as we have seen, the very process of creating employment by means of deficit financing inevitably results in a perpetual shortage of tax collections as compared with government expenditures. The budget thus cannot approach a balance. Moreover, the new philosophy, in one of its manifestations, holds that even in periods of prosperity there must be no reduction in the cash deficit—because this would mean a decrease in the Treasury's "net income-creating" expenditures, with resulting *deflation*. (See pages 40-42.)

In fact, there is nothing in the long history of public finance which indicates that any government, and especially a democratic government, can be depended upon to apply the brakes to credit expansion, when the proper moment has arrived. Always the pressures for continuation along the existing road are powerful and persistent.[52]

It should be recalled here that as a result of long experience with such pressures, the management of *bank credit currency* was, during the course of the nineteenth century, nearly everywhere divorced from political control. It was generally believed at that period that the central banks could, through appropriate credit policies, control the fluctuations of the business cycle. But now that experience has demonstrated that the central banks are powerless either to prevent deflation or to provide an adequate stimulus for recovery and expansion, we have turned to the Treasury as the one agency which can directly affect the volume of purchasing power in the hands of the public.

But the Treasury does not occupy a position of independence comparable to that of the Federal Reserve system as originally conceived and organized. The Treasury is basically an administrative agency. The policies which it executes, both in connection with tax levies and expenditures, are determined by Congress. This fact obviously in-

[52] This is well illustrated by Schacht's failure in Germany in 1938.

volves difficulties from the point of view of developing a scientific, flexible plan of credit control.

To meet this difficulty advocates of control of the economic system through fiscal policy recommend that the power of discretion in both taxation and expenditures be transferred from Congress to the executive branch of the government. The function of Congress would thenceforth be confined to providing lump sum appropriations and to setting certain limitations within which the administration might operate its fiscal program. In connection with expenditures Congress would merely appropriate totals and leave the administration to determine when, where, and how expenditures should be made.[53]

Such a program would obviously constitute a fundamental departure from the financial principles and procedures laid down by the Constitution. To make such a program really effective it would, however, be necessary to go a step further—for with the over-all lump sum appropriation plan Congress might from year to year so change the amounts appropriated as to cripple

[53] Hansen in the *Chicago Journal of Commerce*, June 27, 1942.

the operation of the plan. To assure real freedom of action for the administration a complete delegation of the power to raise and expend money would be necessary.

But even with such a delegation of financial powers the executive branch of the government would not be free from public pressures. Such pressures are now exerted jointly against the Congress and the administration. With Congress eliminated from the financial picture, they would henceforth simply be concentrated on the Executive.

In any case, inflation could not be completely controlled by means of fiscal policy. As has already been shown, fiscal controls do not directly touch certain vital aspects of the problem—those operating from the side of costs. Moreover, history reveals that price inflation frequently occurs by a very different process from that which has thus far been discussed.

2. Inflation by Way of the Foreign Exchanges

The issuance of some 400 millions of *irredeemable* greenback currency during the Civil War led to advances in commodity prices by way of the foreign exchanges. The doubt which existed in the minds of both exporters and importers as to the ultimate value of the greenbacks quickly resulted in their being quoted below par in terms of gold. Stated the other way around, there was a *premium* on gold. Since comparisons with foreign gold currencies were involved, the prices of goods moving in international trade were raised in proportion as our currency depreciated in terms of gold.[54] In turn, the rise in the prices of imported raw materials exerted a direct influence, through rising costs, upon the prices of domestic manufactures. And again the rising wages made necessary by rising prices served to promote further advances in prices by way of the cost side of the equation. In other words, the depreciation of the greenbacks in the exchange markets set in operation the well-known vicious spiral of rising costs, prices, and again costs.

It was by this process also that the devaluation of the dollar in 1933 led to an advance in commodity prices. The prices of articles entering into international trade were directly affected by the changes in the value of the dollar as compared

[54] For a full account of this phenomenon, see Wesley C. Mitchell, *History of the Greenbacks* (1903).

with the monetary units of other countries. And, indirectly, the costs of goods made from imported materials rose somewhat; and again an advance in wage rates was regarded as a necessary part of the process.[55]

Moreover, an inflationary movement proceeding by way of exchange depreciation can be set in motion even when there is no tampering with the monetary standard—when there is merely an uncontrolled expansion of the public debt. When investors lose confidence in a government's ability to maintain financial equilibrium, an effort is always made to transfer investments in that country to safer quarters. American Treasury difficulties in the 1890's were largely due to the withdrawal by foreigners of funds invested in the United States.[56] There was a "flight of capital" away from what had come to be regarded as a danger spot.

Similarly, there may be a flight of domestically-owned capital to safer havens in foreign countries. An excellent illustration of a capital movement of this type is found in the flight from the franc in the middle 1930's, occasioned chiefly by the rapid ex-

[55] For a full account, see Leo Pasvolsky, *Current Monetary Issues* (1933).

[56] See Alexander D. Noyes, *Forty Years of American Finance* (1909), pp. 216-33.

pansion of the public debt and the loss of confidence in the fiscal stability of the government. An accompanying result was the virtual cessation of new investment in private business enterprise.

The stages involved in the process of financial disintegration which ensued have been well summarized by Professor Robert M. Haig of Columbia University, as follows:

> Signs of an exhaustion of borrowing power began to appear in 1934. In connection with the Poincaré stabilization, careful safeguards had been thrown about the Bank of France and these began to make difficulties in connection with the absorption of the treasury paper. The great commercial banks showed a reluctance to increase their holdings of treasury bills when they could not be rediscounted at the Bank of France. The government then brought pressure on the bank to consent to a relaxation of standards and safeguards. In the ensuing struggle the bank lost first its governor, then its safeguards and, ultimately, its character.[57]

Under these conditions the position of the French government's finances went from bad to worse. The situation not only brought about a sharp advance in the prices of commodities, but it also undermined the very foundations of business

[57] "The National Budgets of France, 1928-37," *Proceedings of the Academy of Political Science, 1936-38,* p. 436.

enterprise, employment, and social and political stability.

3. Modern Methods of Control

But does not the foregoing discussion relate to conditions which no longer exist? Has not the abandonment of the gold standard profoundly altered the problem? Do we not now have the means of preventing inflation through the processes which have just been discussed? The answer involves a number of considerations.

The processes which have been described operate, as we have seen, through the foreign exchanges; and in the historical cases cited the exchanges were not subject to rigid control. Under present conditions it would not be possible for any great amount of capital to flee the United States, because the necessary export licenses could not be obtained. Thus this particular danger would seem to be under control.[58]

It remains possible that instead of buying government bonds the public would prefer to try to

[58] The question may be raised in this connection whether in any case investments would be any safer elsewhere than in the United States. Possibly not, though such countries as Britain and the Dominions, Sweden, and even Russia, have shown no disposition to adhere to the new philosophy of public debt.

hedge against commodity price inflation by buying common stock equities, thus producing an inflation of security values. But this might be circum-
vented by closing the stock markets, though to be
sure there would continue to be a very serious
problem of controlling black markets in stocks.
Speculation in securities could probably be completely eliminated only by the levy of such heavy
taxes on corporate earnings that the value of securities would be destroyed. Similar considerations
apply to the commodity exchanges.

Attempts might also be made to buy urban real
estate or farm lands in the hope of being in on the
rise in money values. This might, however, be
checked by universal rent controls, both on urban
and rural properties. Moreover, in the case of farm
properties, the rise in values might be restrained
by rigid controls over the prices of agricultural
products—the farm bloc to the contrary notwithstanding.

The moral of all this is that if we are willing to
apply totalitarian methods of control, inflation
might be largely held in check, even with a constant increase of the public debt. We should have
to control wage rates and farm incomes; we should
have to regulate corporate earnings; we should

have to control investment; we should have to ration commodities; we should have to control rents; we should have to license foreign trade; we should have to supervise, and possibly close, the security and commodity markets. Given regimentation of virtually every phase of economic life, the process of inflation might be held in leash.

The principal advocates of the new philosophy of public debt have, however, expressed themselves as opposed to regimentation, as strongly in favor of the system of free enterprise:

> We do not want the Government to run the whole show. We do not want a totalitarian state. We want freedom of enterprise. . . .[59]

> We shall have in our hands the tools by which we can create a greater measure of economic justice, without sacrificing any of the essential freedoms.[60]

It will be necessary to make a choice. With unlimited debt expansion we cannot prevent inflation without the use of totalitarian methods of control. No compromise or half-way measures can adjust the difficulties. The choice is between regimentation and inflation.

[59] Alvin H. Hansen, *After the War—Full Employment*, National Resources Planning Board, p. 3.
[60] Adolf A. Berle, Jr., *Fortune*, October 1941, p. 102.

The foregoing analysis serves to disclose the gravest danger with which the United States is now confronted. Unable or unwilling to perceive basic inconsistencies, or to choose between clear-cut alternatives, we drift toward the deep financial waters from which there is no return other than through repudiation in one form or another.

VI. THE PUBLIC DEBT ISSUE
AND POSTWAR PLANS

It was stated at the beginning of this analysis that we are here concerned with the crucial issue of the present time and that, until this issue is settled, no unified plans for postwar reconstruction can be formulated. This is simply because government financial policy is of underlying and permeating significance.

We use the term *issue* rather than *problem* because of the phenomenon of fundamentally divergent conceptions as to the economic significance of the public debt. If, as in former times, all were agreed that the huge debt constitutes a serious economic problem, that its growth must be restrained as much as possible in times of national emergency, and that it must be gradually reduced to manageable proportions after the emergency passes, we would have a very different *problem* of budget balancing on our hands. But when, as now, the view is widely held in influential circles that a constantly expanding public debt is indispensable to national prosperity, that the only means of maintaining full employment is by continuing postwar public expenditures on a plane perhaps comparable to that of the war period, we have an *issue* of public policy—an issue of crucial importance. Unless the issue is first settled there can be no solution of the problem.[61]

The preservation of fiscal stability is indispensable to the maintenance of monetary stability and a freely functioning foreign exchange system. It is indispensable to the prevention of inflation with its distorting effects on the price and wage structure, and thus to the maintenance of social and political stability. Uncertainty over fiscal policies is a powerful deterrent to investment and capital expansion under private auspices. Fears of an ultimate breakdown of government credit, of inflation, and of eventual repudiation in one form or another, serve inevitably to discourage long-term capital commitments. In consequence, unemployment continues; and in consequence of this there is continuing and increasing need for public assistance. Thus, the drift toward an ever-expanding scale of public expenditures and of public enterprise continues—even though there ~~were~~ *Maybe* no responsible groups in the United States in favor of collectivism.

[61] The problems involved in achieving fiscal stability in the postwar world will constitute the subject of other Brookings Institution investigations.

Private enterprise is now endeavoring to formulate plans for the reabsorption of returning soldiers and war workers after the war and for the maintenance of a permanently high level of employment. The goals desired will not, however, be realized unless there is a solid financial foundation on which to build. We will not have a sound basis on which to build constructive plans for postwar industrial rehabilitation and expansion until the prevailing conflict of views is eliminated.

The government likewise is now engaged in the formulation of plans designed not only to furnish adequate employment immediately after the war but also to lay the foundations for a stable and progressive national and international economic system. But the conflicting views now prevailing within the government with respect to the public debt make unified planning virtually impossible.

The situation may be illustrated by the two most important plans for the postwar world thus far presented by government agencies.

In the international field the Treasury Department has suggested as the foundation stone on which to reconstruct investment and trade throughout the world, an international currency system tied to a new gold standard. In the domestic field, the National Resources Planning Board has outlined a two-fold program, involving extensive public works and comprehensive social security. But since this Board is committed to the theory that national prosperity and national income are largely dependent upon the "government's contribution to purchasing power" through deficit financing, it is deemed unnecessary to be seriously concerned about the costs involved in realizing objectives which all agree are desirable. The resulting increase in the public debt is regarded as in the nature of a national asset rather than a national liability.

If the philosophy underlying the National Resources Planning Board's program is accepted as a basis for domestic reconstruction, the Treasury's program for international reconstruction is certain to fail. Unless a stable system of public finance is maintained in the United States, and also in other countries, the foundation stone for international reconstruction will rest on quicksand.